Date Due

JE 10 03		
JA 2 4 '04		
FE 08 05		
OC 08 '07		

Healthy Eating

Perspectives on Physical Health

by Susan R. Gregson

Consultant:
Lora A. Sporny, EdD, RD
Adjunct Associate Professor of Nutrition
and Education
Teachers College, Columbia University

LifeMatters
an imprint of Capstone Press
Mankato, Minnesota

LifeMatters Books are published by Capstone Press
PO Box 669 • 151 Good Counsel Drive • Mankato, Minnesota 56002
http://www.capstone-press.com

Printed in the United States of America

Library of Congress Cataloging-in-Publication Data
Gregson, Susan R.
     Healthy eating / by Susan R. Gregson.
            p.   cm.—(Perspectives on physical health)
     Includes bibliographical references and index.
     Summary: Discusses how different foods are used in our bodies and how to make healthy eating a part of one's lifestyle.
     ISBN 0-7368-0420-X (book)—ISBN 0-7368-0438-2 (series)
     1. Nutrition—Juvenile literature. 2. Health—Juvenile literature. [1. Nutrition 2. Health.] I. Title. II. Series.
     RA784 .G76 2000
     613.2—dc21
                                         99-055019
                                         CIP

Staff Credits
Rebecca Aldridge, Judy L. Stewart, editors; Adam Lazar, designer; Jodi Theisen, photo researcher

Photo Credits
Cover: Stock Market/©Michael Keller
FPG International/©Robert Reiff, 15; ©Elizabeth Simpson, 26; © Telegraph Colour Library, 28; ©Michael Hart, 34; ©George Gibbons, 48; ©Gary Buss, 58
Index Stock Photography/7, 8
Photo Network/©Esbin-Anderson, 39
PNI/©Digital Vision, 12; RubberBall, 33
Unicorn Stock Photos/©Jeff Greenberg, 44; ©Doug Adams, 57
Uniphoto/©Frank Sizeman, 17; ©Michael A. Keller, 18; ©Bob Daemmrich, 40; ©Llewellyn, 42; ©J.B. Smith, 51

A 0 9 8 7 6 5 4 3 2 1

Table of Contents

Chapter Overview

The body needs a variety of foods for energy.

The body turns food into energy in three steps. These steps are digestion, absorption, and metabolism.

Calories are a measure of the energy that food gives the body.

Chapter 1

Body Basics

Steve can't open his locker. He has tried the combination three

STEVE, AGE 16

times. He smacks the locker door with his hand. Steve's friend Barry walks up and asks what's wrong. "Nothing," Steve says loudly. Barry frowns at his friend and starts to walk away. Steve turns and says, "Wait. Sorry I bit your head off, man." Steve explains that he missed lunch while making up a test, and now he is starving. Barry pulls an orange out of his backpack and hands it to Steve. "Here, eat this, and I'll open your locker. I have some granola bars down at the gym. You can have those before hockey practice." Steve peels the orange. "Thanks, I owe you."

The body needs the right mix of foods to stay healthy and work its best. A diet is what a person eats each day. A balanced diet includes many nutritious foods from the major food groups. A balanced diet helps people feel energetic. It also helps people to look their best and fight illness. A stomach filled with foods high in added sugars and fats can make people moody, grumpy, and tired. How can food do all this? Here's what happens after food is popped into the mouth.

Food—Another Word for Energy

The food you eat needs to be broken down into little pieces. Then your body can use it as energy. The body takes three steps to turn what you eat into energy. These steps are called digestion, absorption, and metabolism.

Digestion

The body breaks down food during digestion, which begins as soon as food enters the mouth. Chewing food breaks it down. The chemicals in saliva, or spit, also begin to break down food.

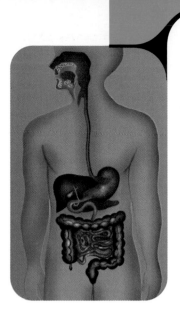

When a person swallows food, it travels through the esophagus to the stomach. The esophagus is a long tube between the throat and the stomach. In the stomach are chemicals that break down the food even more. These chemicals are called stomach acids and enzymes. Food then moves from the stomach to the small intestine, a long, coiled part of the digestive system.

Absorption

The next process is absorption. This is the process of moving nutrients from the small intestine into the bloodstream. Nutrients are parts of food that the body needs to work well. The bloodstream delivers nutrients to the body's cells.

Metabolism

The process your body uses to change nutrients into energy is called metabolism. After absorption, the body's cells take in the nutrients from the bloodstream. Then the nutrients are converted to energy the cells can use. As nutrients are used, wastes are created and removed by the cells. The body gets rid of wastes every time people exhale, or breathe out, sweat, and go to the bathroom.

Nicole has a busy schedule. She hangs out with friends,

NICOLE, AGE 14

does schoolwork, watches her little brother, and plays soccer. Sometimes she goes hours between meals. Nicole's doctor told her about eating healthy snacks to help keep her going. Nicole puts carrots, raisins, and popcorn in her backpack on busy days. Dr. Coakley also suggested that Nicole write down each night what she ate all day. He showed her how to count the number of calories in her food. He told her how to plan her meals and snacks using different food groups. This way, Nicole eats the right mix of foods. This gives her body the right number of calories.

Calories

A calorie measures how much energy a food gives the body. More calories mean more energy. Extra calories not needed for energy are stored in the body as fat. Teens usually need between 2,200 and 2,500 calories each day. The number of calories you need depends on how active you are and whether you are male or female. Boys generally need more calories because they have more muscle mass.

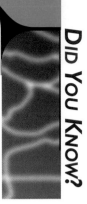
Most experts agree that the average American diet should be about 2,000 calories a day. These calories should come mostly from nutritious foods. Teens and active adults may need up to 2,500 calories.

The body needs foods that have a lot of nutrients, not just a lot of calories. Some foods such as chocolate cake are loaded with calories. However, they do not have many nutrients. Other foods such as raw vegetables have a lot of nutrients but not a lot of calories.

Calories are just a guide to help a person eat the right amounts of food. Healthy eating does not mean simply counting calories. It means thinking about both the calories and nutrients in foods. Healthy eating also means eating a variety of nutritious foods. Other guides can help people plan a balanced diet. Some of these guides are discussed in Chapter 4.

Points to Consider

Do you think that it is true that people are what they eat? Why or why not?

Name some foods that are high in calories but that do not have a lot of nutrients in them.

Can you think of a food that you eat every day that has a lot of nutrients?

Chapter Overview

The six main types of nutrients that the body needs are carbohydrates, proteins, fats, vitamins, minerals, and water.

A person needs a balanced amount of nutrients for good health.

The healthiest diet is mostly carbohydrates and some proteins and fats.

The body gets its energy from carbohydrates, proteins, and fats.

Vitamins, minerals, and water help the body to use the energy from food.

Chapter 2

The Super Six Nutrients You Need

The body needs six types of nutrients to live and be healthy. A person has to consume these nutrients. These super six nutrients are carbohydrates, proteins, fats, vitamins, minerals, and water. Carbohydrates, proteins, and fats give the body energy. Vitamins, minerals, and water do not provide energy, but they help the body to use the energy in food. People need smaller amounts of vitamins and minerals than carbohydrates, proteins, and fats. The body needs plenty of water each day to replace the water it loses.

Carbohydrates

The terms *sugars* and *starches* refer to carbohydrates, also called carbs or carbos for short. Grain foods such as bread, cereal, pasta, and tortillas, along with beans, fruits, vegetables, and milk, all contain carbohydrates. Even candy bars, cake, and soda contain carbohydrates. In fact, all foods except meats, poultry, fish, and eggs contain carbohydrates. The body breaks down carbohydrates into sugars. These sugars give your body its energy. Extra sugars are stored in the liver and muscle. If too much sugar is in the body, it is turned into fat. The body uses stored sugar for energy when it hasn't had food for a while. Most of the foods people eat each day should contain carbohydrates.

This doesn't mean people should load up on brownies, cookies, and cola for their carbohydrates. These types of foods contain mostly sugars and refined starches added by processors. These foods are basically carbohydrate calories with few other nutrients. People may call them sweets, junk food, or empty calories. Too much added sugar and refined starches give a quick burst of energy that soon drops and leaves a person feeling tired.

While it is okay to eat added sugars and refined starches occasionally, people need naturally present sugars and unrefined starches every day. Foods with naturally present sugars are fruits, 100-percent fruit juices, some vegetables, and milk. Foods with unrefined starches are whole grains, whole-grain breads, cereals, pastas, vegetables, nuts, and beans. The added benefit of eating these foods is that they also contain the other nutrients needed for good health. Except for milk and juice, all of these foods have fiber. This is a part of food that the body cannot fully digest. Fiber is important because it helps foods move through the digestive system and keeps this system healthy.

Proteins

Proteins not only provide energy but also build muscles and repair body tissues. In fact, the body first uses proteins to do this. Then, the body stores leftover proteins as body fat. Protein-rich foods include meat, poultry, fish, eggs, milk, and beans. Grains, breads, cereals, pasta, vegetables, and nuts also contain proteins. About 15 percent of the calories we eat should come from proteins.

Proteins are made of building blocks called amino acids. There are about 20 different amino acids used to make proteins. The body can make all but nine of these amino acids. People have to eat these nine amino acids in proteins to stay healthy.

Myth: Fish is food for the brain, or "brain food."

Fact: Fish has many nutrients people need to eat to be healthy. In fact, fish can help the blood flow smoothly and can boost the immune system to fight infections. It also can lower the amount of cholesterol and fat in the blood. However, fish does not have a magical effect on learning.

Proteins that have all nine of these amino acids are called complete proteins. All animal foods such as meat, fish, eggs, and milk have complete proteins. Some plant foods such as soybeans and tofu have complete proteins. Combining plant foods with each other or with animal foods also provides the needed amino acids. For example, beans with rice, peanut butter on bread, or cereal with milk gives people complete proteins.

Fats

Fats provide energy and help the body use vitamins. Fats are in all cells of the body. People need just a little fat in their diet. Extra fat that is not needed for energy is stored under the skin and around the organs. Calories from fat are stored as body fat more easily than calories from other nutrients. Less than 30 percent of a person's daily calories should come from fats. Some people should eat less fat than this, especially people who wish to lower their risk for heart attacks. Too much fat increases the chances of becoming obese and getting heart disease and some kinds of cancer.

However, not enough fat in the diet may leave a person with little energy. The body also may not be able to use certain vitamins. Too little fat in the diet can lead to dry skin, damaged hair, and stomach problems. For women, it can lead to menstrual problems. Menstruation is the monthly discharge of blood, fluids, and tissue from the utcrus in nonpregnant females.

Most meats, cheeses, french fries, and chips are foods high in fat. Salad dressing, nuts, and avocados contain fats, too. Two main types of fats are saturated and unsaturated. Saturated fats come from meats, cheeses, ice creams, fried foods, and store-bought baked goods. They usually are solid at room temperature. Less than a third of the fats a person eats should be saturated. Saturated fats are not healthy. They increase the risk of many disorders.

Unsaturated fats come mostly from plant foods and, if eaten in moderation, are good for health. Usually they are liquid at room temperature. Examples of foods that have unsaturated fats are nuts, seeds, salad dressings, avocados, olives, and fish.

Chi-I's favorite meal was a
double bacon cheeseburger with
fries and a chocolate shake. When Chi-I went for his physical
to play varsity baseball this year, his doctor did a blood test.
The test showed that Chi-I's cholesterol was too high. The
doctor encouraged Chi-I to keep playing sports because
exercise helps lower cholesterol. She also asked Chi-I to eat
fewer fatty foods. She said a burger and fries were okay as a
treat, but he shouldn't eat them every day. Chi-I promised to
eat more lean meats and to not eat fried foods as often. He
didn't want cholesteral and fat clogging his arteries.

CHI-I, AGE 16

Cholesterol

Cholesterol is a waxy substance found only in foods that come
from animals. Cholesterol is found in every cell of the body.
Although it is not a nutrient, the body needs some cholesterol.
In fact, the liver can make all the cholesterol that the body
needs. However, too much cholesterol in the blood can clog the
blood vessels. Clogged blood vessels can block blood flow to
the heart and brain. Over time, this can cause a heart attack or
stroke. Too much cholesterol from animal foods can increase
blood cholesterol. However, the chief cause of elevated blood
cholesterol is eating too much saturated fat. Saturated fat tells
the liver to overproduce cholesterol.

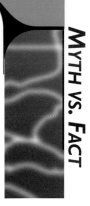
Myth: People should not eat foods that contain fat or cholesterol.

Fact: The body needs unsaturated fats from foods. The body does not need saturated fats and cholesterol from foods, but it is okay to eat some. The liver makes the cholesterol the body needs. Fat provides energy, and cholesterol works in the body's cells. Too much fat and cholesterol, though, can lead to long-term health problems. Such problems may include becoming overweight, which can lead to heart disease and diabetes.

Vitamins

Vitamins are good for the cells and help the blood clot. Vitamins are substances found in all healthy foods.

Vitamins A, D, E, and K dissolve in fats and are stored easily in the body. These vitamins help keep hair and eyes healthy. They also keep bones and teeth strong. Vitamin A is in foods such as milk, carrots, and spinach. Vitamin D is contained in milk and fish. Vegetable oils have vitamin E. Vitamin K is in green vegetables, soybeans, and bran. Taking too many vitamin supplements, or pills, may give a person too much vitamin A and D.

Vitamin C and the eight different B vitamins dissolve in water. Soaking foods that contain these vitamins too long can wash away their nutrients. Vitamins B and C pass through the body quickly. Therefore, people need to eat foods with these vitamins every day. The B vitamins protect skin and nerves, help digestion, and protect the body from illness. The body uses vitamin C to form bones and teeth and to fight infections. Meats, cereals, whole grains, green vegetables, peanut butter, bread, and eggs contain the B vitamins. Citrus fruits, tomatoes, broccoli, red bell peppers, and potatoes have vitamin C.

Minerals

Minerals are elements formed in the earth. Minerals are important for good health. They help to keep fluids in your body balanced and add structure to tissues. Three important minerals are calcium, iron, and zinc. These three minerals help a teen's body grow. Most teens need to eat more of these minerals. Calcium helps bones and teeth stay strong. Red blood cells need iron to carry oxygen from the lungs to all cells of the body. Zinc is needed for growth, sexual development, and wound healing. Calcium is in milk, yogurt, cheese, beans, almonds, and blackstrap molasses. Iron is found in meats, beans, eggs, cereals, and breads. Zinc is plentiful in meats, beans, yogurt, nuts, and seeds.

Water

The human body is about 60 percent water. Almost everything that the body does involves water. For example, water helps the body flush out wastes and helps maintain body temperature. A good rule of thumb is to drink eight 8-ounce glasses of water every day. People also can get water from some foods such as soups, juices, fruits, and vegetables.

Kimberly drinks eight glasses of water each day. She fills up a half-gallon container of water in the morning and drinks it throughout the day. When the plastic container is empty, she knows her body has gotten enough water for the day. Kimberly usually knows when she has forgotten to drink enough water. Her skin gets dry, and her urine is dark yellow and has a strong odor.

KIMBERLY, AGE 17

Points to Consider

The next time you eat something, think about the nutrients the food is bringing to your body. Could you add something to what you are eating to make your diet healthier?

How can you make sure the carbohydrates you eat include naturally present sugars and unrefined starches? What are some foods that provide these carbohydrates?

What are some foods that might cause waxy, fatty buildup in the arteries if eaten too often?

What are some things you could do to make sure you drink enough water each day?

Chapter Overview

What teens eat affects them both now and later.

Teens who do not eat right may be tired or overweight.

A lifetime of unhealthy eating can lead to serious illness. It can result in diabetes, heart disease, stroke, high blood pressure, some types of cancer, and arthritis.

Chapter **3**

A Balanced Diet for a Balanced Body

It's pretty simple. People cannot live without food. People can live without certain kinds of food, though. Someone once said that there is no junk food, just junk diets. It is okay to eat triple-fudge brownies or barbecue potato chips once in a while. However, a healthy diet has these foods in it only sometimes. Mostly, the body needs foods that are high in nutrients and low in calories.

What people eat affects how they feel all day and all their life. It is important to eat foods that give the body the nutrients it needs. Without these nutrients, people may have less energy, hair that is less shiny, and skin that is less soft. Without these nutrients, the body systems cannot work. Unhealthy diets can cause problems with the brain, nervous system, muscles, and with growth.

"My favorite snack is a chocolate bar, but I save this snack for special times. Usually I eat graham crackers or a bagel with a glass of milk or low-fat cheese for a snack. After a good snack, I feel ready to baby-sit the neighbor's kids. Sometimes if I just grab a candy bar, I feel really tired before my baby-sitting job is done. The candy tastes great. The crackers and milk taste good, too. But I definitely think I feel better and stay less hungry longer if I eat the healthier snack."—Alana, age 15

The Present

If you ignore your body, it will probably slow down. If you skip breakfast, your stomach may growl two hours later. That growling is your body's way of saying, "I need food to work." If you skip meals and snacks, you may be grumpy and tired by day's end.

Teens who eat too much food that is high in fat and calories may weigh more than they should. Right now, that may mean they don't feel comfortable with how they look. These teens may have trouble breathing after walking to class. In the future, these teens could become adults who have serious health problems.

The Future

Teens may have a hard time thinking about the future. So much is going on in their life today. Learning to eat right as a teen, however, can help a teen to become a stronger, healthier adult. It may mean a longer, happier life.

Teens who don't eat right probably will not eat right later in life. That can mean serious trouble such as diabetes, stroke, and heart disease. Unhealthy eating also can cause high blood pressure, some types of cancer, and arthritis.

Such diseases don't just sneak up on people. They happen after years of not eating right and not exercising enough. However, signs of these diseases often occur early in life. For example, researchers in one study examined the bodies of teens killed in car accidents. These teens already had waxy, fatty deposits in the arteries that pump blood around the heart. And recently, many overweight teens who don't exercise are developing type 2 diabetes. Before now, this disease was seen rarely in anyone younger than 40.

In fact, by age 12 nearly 70 percent of children have fat and cholesterol building up in their coronary, or heart, arteries. All the saturated fat and cholesterol in an American teen's diet continues to build up in the arteries. Arteries with waxy, fatty deposits are one of the earliest signs of possible future heart disease and heart attacks. More people in the United States die each year from heart attacks than from anything else.

Points to Consider

Can you think of some foods that you eat regularly that your body does not need to live?

What are some signs that your body is getting enough nutrients?

What are some things that may happen if a person does not eat a balanced diet early in life?

Chapter Overview

Dietary guidelines and food guides provided by the government can help people create a healthy diet.

Food packages list daily values. These values show the amounts of important nutrients that people should eat daily.

Vegetarian diets can be quite healthy if foods are picked carefully.

Chapter **4**
Help for Healthy Eating

What you have read so far about the nutrients your body needs may sound hard to remember. You may wonder how to determine the amounts of the super six nutrients to eat each day. Several guides can help.

Dietary Guidelines

The U.S. and Canadian governments have dietary guidelines for healthy eating. Doctors, other health professionals, and schools use the guidelines to teach people about healthy eating. The guidelines are on the next page. They are pretty easy to remember.

1. Balance the food you eat with exercise. Try to maintain or, only if necessary, improve your weight.

2. Choose a diet with plenty of grains, vegetables, and fruits.

3. Pick a diet low in fat, especially saturated fat, and cholesterol.

4. Eat a lot of different foods.

5. Eat foods with little salt, added sugars, or caffeine in them. Caffeine can cause nervousness and water and calcium loss.

The Food Guide Pyramid

The U.S. government created the Food Guide Pyramid to help people make dietary guidelines a part of their life. Many food packages, such as a box of cereal, display the chart.

The pyramid is made of layers that show suggested servings for a particular food group. The bottom of the pyramid is made up of breads, cereals, and grains. The next level consists of vegetables and fruits. Combined, these levels include most of the carbohydrate-rich foods that are essential for energy. A slightly smaller level that represents dairy and meats, poultry, fish, eggs, and beans is next. These foods help maintain a strong, well-functioning body. As the size of the layer indicates, you need small amounts of these foods each day.

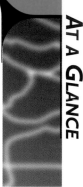

Here are the daily servings experts recommend for active teens from the Food Guide Pyramid.

	Number of servings for teen boys	Number of servings for teen girls
Breads/grains	11	9
Vegetables	5	4
Fruits	4	3
Milk foods	2 to 3	2 to 3
Meats and meat substitutes	3 servings or up to 7 ounces	2 servings or up to 6 ounces

The tip of the pyramid is for foods with fats, oils, and added sugars. These foods should be eaten only occasionally.

The pyramid lists the number of servings people should eat each day to get all the needed nutrients. The serving numbers apply to most people. Serving sizes may be smaller than what people might eat normally. For example, many people eat two slices of bread in one sandwich. This counts as two servings on the pyramid. Some teens need more foods from one part of the pyramid or another. These may be teens who play sports, are really active, or are having a growth spurt. Nutrition experts say teens should use the higher serving numbers the pyramid lists.

Canadian Guide to Healthy Eating

People in Canada use a chart that looks different from the Food Guide Pyramid. The Canadian Food Guide to Healthy Eating looks like a rainbow of foods. The chart works like the pyramid. It shows what kinds of food make up a healthy diet. It also shows how much of the main nutrients people should try to eat daily.

Daily Values

Daily values are another guideline. Daily values help people compare the amount of nutrients in one serving of different foods. Labels on food packages list daily values for many nutrients. Chapter 7 talks more about food labels. Daily values are based on a 2,000-calorie diet. Teens may need more than the listed daily value for some nutrients, such as calcium.

Soledad is a vegetarian. She uses the Food Guide Pyramid.

SOLEDAD, AGE 18

However, Soledad's pyramid has changes in the meat, poultry, fish, dry beans, eggs, and nuts group. Instead, her pyramid lists legumes, nuts, seeds, and meat alternatives. Soledad doesn't carry the chart with her. She has a mental picture of it. Before dinner, she thinks about what she has eaten. Soledad tries to eat foods at dinner that she didn't have enough of that day.

Being a Vegetarian

Vegetarianism, or having a meatless diet, can be a healthy way to eat. Teens who are vegetarians still need the protein, iron, zinc, and other nutrients that meats contain. Different plant foods can be eaten together to get these same nutrients. One example is eating iron-rich cereal with milk and drinking a glass of orange juice. The vitamin C in the juice helps get more iron into the body. A doctor or dietitian can adjust food guides for vegetarians. A dietitian has education and training in healthy eating and foods.

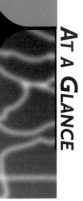
Different types of vegetarians are:

Vegan: does not eat or wear any animal foods or products, not even something like honey

Lacto-vegetarian: does not eat fish, chicken, eggs, and meat, but does eat milk foods

Lacto-ovo vegetarian: does not eat meat, poultry, and fish, but does eat eggs and milk foods. This type of vegetarian is the most common type in the United States.

Whom Can You Call?

A doctor, school nurse, or health teacher can give you information about healthy eating. This person can give you details about guides for healthy eating and exercise.

The U.S. Department of Agriculture (USDA) and the U.S. Department of Health and Human Services (USDHHS) keep track of how and what Americans eat. Health Canada programs cover healthy eating in Canada. These agencies have a lot of good information about healthy eating. These and other helpful organizations are listed in the back of this book.

Points to Consider

Do you think the Food Guide Pyramid is a good illustration for healthy eating? Why or why not? Can you think of other ways to illustrate healthy eating?

Which of the five healthy eating guidelines do you have the hardest time following? What is something that you could do to meet that guideline?

Do you think being a vegetarian is easy? Why or why not?

Chapter Overview

Many people are not happy with their weight. Some people may eat less, or diet, to try to lose weight.

Fad diets come and go. They usually promise to help people lose a lot of weight or to lose weight quickly.

The surest way to look and feel your best is to balance a healthy diet with exercise.

Some people have emotional problems related to body image and food. They may try to control their eating in an unhealthy way.

Chapter **5**

Unhealthy Eating

Dieting for Weight Loss

Until now, the word *diet* in this book meant what a person eats daily—a healthy diet, a balanced diet. However, the words *diet* and *dieting* also mean what people do to lose weight. Used in this way, diet means restricting calories. Many teens and adults do not eat right or exercise enough. Many people struggle to control their weight. Some studies show that the majority of people in the United States are overweight. This means most Americans have more body fat than is healthy. Some people want to be thinner, so they try eating less to lose weight.

By age 6, nearly 40 percent of girls in the United States have said they want to be thinner. By age 9, almost half of girls in the United States have dieted once. By age 16, 45 percent have tried a fad diet and 15 percent take diet pills regularly.

Many different diet books, programs, and drugs are supposed to help people lose weight. A friend may be on a diet of only fruit. Your mom may be on a diet that is mostly protein instead of carbohydrates. Your uncle may drink nutrient shakes three times a day. No one seems to agree on which diet method works best. Most of these diets promise fast and easy weight loss.

Isaac is on his third diet. He went on his first diet when he

ISAAC, AGE 13

was 10. That was because his aunt told him he had chubby cheeks. Isaac only eats green vegetables on this new diet. He read in a magazine that his favorite actor lost 15 pounds on the diet. Isaac has lost a little weight, but he is tired and has headaches. He is not sure how long he can stay on this diet.

Just a Fad

Medical experts agree that dieting rarely works. Most diets are called fad diets. These diets come and go like the latest fashions. They can be dangerous to a teen's health. Often, they limit certain foods that the body still needs. People can become weak, tired, and angry on a fad diet. The diets usually promise to help people lose a lot of weight quickly. If they worked as promised, however, there would be fewer overweight people. Instead, the number of overweight people in the United States keeps growing.

The Best Method

The best diets are programs that teach people to eat a variety of foods. The programs are based on the information from government guidelines. A good program includes eating nutritious foods combined with exercising several times a week.

Following a program of healthy eating and regular exercise can be difficult. Eating nutritious foods and exercising takes time. In our fast-paced culture, people often try shortcuts. They may try diets that work for a while. However, the weight usually comes back. Sometimes people gain even more weight after a diet.

Eating Disorders

TASHA, AGE 16

Tasha thinks she is too fat. Her family and friends keep telling her to eat more. But Tasha looks in the mirror every morning and sees fat around her waist. Tasha tries not to eat anything with fat or carbohydrates in it. She thinks these food have too many calories. Tasha's mom often insists that Tasha eat dinner with the family. When this happens, Tasha makes herself throw up after she eats. Tasha wants to look like the model on the magazine cover taped to her bedroom mirror.

Tasha has an eating disorder. An eating disorder is an emotional problem with the way a person thinks about food. This causes people with eating disorders to misuse food. They either eat too much or too little. An eating disorder can be extreme dieting. This type of disorder is called anorexia nervosa or anorexia. Sometimes extreme dieting is combined with too much exercise.

Some people eat large amounts of food and then throw it up. They may take drugs called laxatives that make them go to the bathroom a lot. Eating a lot, called bingeing, and then throwing up, or purging, are signs of the eating disorder bulimia.

Sometimes the opposite happens, and a person may overeat and become overweight. This disorder is usually called overeating or compulsive eating.

People who have eating disorders can get sick and even die. Both males and females can have eating disorders. However, girls are more likely than boys to have them. People who have eating disorders often need medical attention to make sure they get the nutrients they need. More importantly, they may need professional help to recover emotionally from an eating disorder.

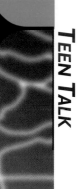

"My sister had to drag me to the doctor. I just could not admit that I had bulimia. I have been seeing a counselor now for almost three years. There are days when I still want to throw up what I have eaten. But there are more days when I don't think about food too much. It's really important to get professional help, though. Friends and family just aren't enough."
—Cindy, age 17

Eating disorders and fad diets can be life threatening. If you think you might have an eating disorder or if you know someone who might, tell a trusted adult. Talk with your doctor or school counselor if you are concerned about your weight. If your doctor thinks you need to lose weight, he or she will tell you. You also can look up *Psychologist* or *Psychiatrist* in the phone book. Many mental health professionals work with patients who have eating disorders.

Points to Consider

What would you say if a friend of average weight said he or she was going on a diet?

What do you think would happen if a person ate only fruit for a month to lose weight?

Why do you think teens can have eating disorders?

What would you do if you thought a friend had an eating disorder?

Chapter Overview

Feelings, family, and friends can influence what you choose to eat.

Where people eat and the way they live also influence food choices.

The media send mixed messages about food and eating. The media advertise unhealthy food but do not show the consequences of unhealthy eating.

Chapter **6**

Influences on Your Eating

A lot of things can influence what people eat. Many people don't realize why they eat certain foods. Feelings, family, and friends all play a role in what people eat. Surroundings, lifestyle, or how you live, and the media also affect food choices.

Feelings and Food

Food can make people feel loved and comforted. Eating to make sad, angry, or nervous feelings go away is called emotional eating. Some people eat a favorite food when they are upset. This sometimes keeps people from facing their problems. They eat to hide their feelings. Sometimes people who eat because of emotions eat too much and become overweight. Chapter 8 talks about some ways to lessen the effect emotions have on food choices.

"After a bad day at school, I used to grab a bag of chocolate chip cookies from the kitchen. I would eat the whole bag by myself. The cookies reminded me of the ones my mom used to have waiting for me after school. She did that before she started working full-time again. After taking my health class with Ms. Finch, though, I learned about better snacks. Now I come home and eat yogurt or carrots. I don't let my emotions affect my food choices anymore."— Matthew, age 15

Family and Food

Family plays a strong part in what people choose to eat. When you were younger, parents or other family members probably chose your food. As you got older, they may have given you more say about what to eat.

What you learned from family can affect what you eat today. For example, one teen's family may offer a variety of nutritious foods at meals. It is likely the teen will choose nutritious foods when away from home. Another teen's family may prepare high-fat, high-calorie food. That teen is likely to eat such food as an adult.

Some families may make teens eat everything they are served. These teens may have learned to eat even when they are no longer hungry. Some teens may eat to make other people happy. That could mean stuffing in the last bite of cake, even if the person didn't want it.

Friends and Food

Manuel, Justin, and Len had a
few minutes before baseball
MANUEL, AGE 16
practice. "I'm starving," Justin said as he ran to the vending
machines and bought a candy bar. Len opened a bag of potato
chips. Manuel pulled a lunch bag from his backpack. Justin
teased Manuel about what he was eating. "Manny, why are
you eating rabbit food?" he asked, pointing to Manuel's
carrots and sweet cherry tomatoes. Manuel laughed but slid
the veggies back into his backpack. He hopped up and headed
to the vending machines.

Friends may make you feel good or bad about what you eat.
Friends can have a lot of influence if you let them. It may be hard
to eat nutritious food when other people around you are eating
high-fat snacks and sweets. You might think about eating the same
thing. It's okay to eat those snacks occasionally. However, eating
right means balancing cookies with more nutritious food later.

Instead of putting the healthy food away, Manuel could have brought enough for everyone to eat. His friends might have skipped the vending machines just to save money. Friends may find that they like snacks such as vegetables, popcorn, and crackers.

Often we spend time with friends by celebrating with food. This is called social eating. For example, dating often involves dining out. Friday nights may be pizza night with the team. You may eat junk food just because everyone else is eating it. You may eat because you do not want to hurt anyone's feelings.

Learning to eat right means finding nutritious foods even when you are with other people. Most get-togethers have something nutritious. You can bring something healthy yourself. On your next date, skip the burgers and pack a picnic. If you eat pizza with friends after a movie, grab slices with veggies on them.

Where You Are and What You Eat

Your surroundings can affect what is available to eat. Home, school, and dining out all present different options.

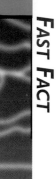
Home

Your home may or may not have a large selection of foods. You could offer to help your parents do the grocery shopping. Then you could select foods that are low in fat, especially saturated fat, and calories. Fill the refrigerator and pantry with whole-grain cereals, crackers, breads, tortillas, beans, vegetables, and fruits.

Experiment with low-fat dips for the vegetables, crackers, and tortillas. Salsa and seasoned mashed beans make tasty dips. Cut up the fruit into bite-size chunks and make a mixed fruit salad. Sprinkle sunflower seeds or honey-toasted wheat germ on top for a sweet and crunchy snack. Mix some low-fat or nonfat plain or vanilla yogurt with fruit, and drizzle molasses across the top. Peeled frozen bananas and frozen grapes and berries are cool treats on a hot day. Blend frozen fruits with milk or yogurt for a shake. Try frozen peas and corn right out of the freezer.

If nutritious foods are on hand, you are more likely to eat them. Teens in one survey enjoyed healthier snacks if the foods were right there and ready to eat. As long as healthy snacks were handy, they liked them just as much as chips, cookies, and candy.

Rachel and Adam usually **RACHEL AND ADAM, AGES 15 AND 17** take turns packing their lunches each night before school. That way they each only have to do it a few times a week. When they don't pack lunch, they buy fresh fruit in the cafeteria. Adam and Rachel keep nutritious snacks in their locker, so they can avoid the vending machines. Friends look for Rachel and Adam between classes to raid their locker for munchies.

School

School may present a healthy eating challenge. Teens who don't pack a lunch may eat foods in the cafeteria that are not the best choices. Instead of going for the fries and ice cream, pick a green vegetable and fruit for dessert. If you do have a high-fat lunch, try to get fruits and vegetables in at dinner. School vending machines usually are loaded with candy, cookies, and sugary drinks. You can save money by carrying healthy snacks in your backpack. Fresh fruit, granola bars, dry cereal, popcorn, and pretzels are just a few ideas.

One medium order of fries from a fast-food restaurant has nearly 25 percent of a teen's daily fat limit.

FAST FACT

Restaurants and Fast Food

Restaurants offer many flavorful dishes. People may order something that looks delicious, even if it is loaded with calories. Fast-food restaurants are especially tempting. More than 20 percent of the population eats at a fast-food restaurant every day. Fast-food restaurants often have meal deals. These include huge servings of fries, soda, and burgers or fried chicken. Many menu items at fast-food restaurants have too much fat, salt, and sugar. However, almost all fast-food restaurants offer salads, baked or grilled chicken sandwiches, and smaller food servings.

Lifestyle and Food Choices

People today live differently than families did just 10 years ago. Today's teen may not have a parent around during the day to help make good food choices. Schedules are so busy that people often eat at restaurants. Many families do not eat meals together because of school, work, and activities.

People feel they have little time to eat right, exercise, and get enough sleep. Eating competes with other activities for our time. A recent survey showed that 64 percent of people eat while doing something else such as watching television, reading, or working. The most important thing today seems to be convenience, or how easy it is to do something.

Healthy eating usually is considered too hard to do every day. Many people eat foods that are already prepared. Prepared foods usually are high in fat. In many places, the easiest snacks to get are candy, cookies, and chips.

Many people eat on the run or in their cars. Fast-food restaurants are a popular place to eat, especially for teens. These restaurants offer a lot of food at a fair price. Snacks become meals. Fast food is almost always fatty food.

These habits make it easy to eat unhealthy foods. The eating habits of this "grab-and-go" lifestyle may have been learned over years. Chapter 7 talks about changing unhealthy eating habits, even in a fast-paced world. Chapter 8 offers tips that can help anyone make healthy eating a part of his or her life.

Media Madness

The media include television, newspapers, magazines, radio, and movies. When it comes to food, the media deliver a mixed message. Advertisements encourage people to buy high-fat, high-calorie foods. A study of 222 food ads on Saturday morning TV showed that only 8 were for nutritious foods.

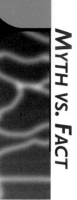
Myth: People in magazines look like everyone else.

Fact: Female magazine models are 9 percent taller and 23 percent thinner than the average woman. Photographs are retouched to remove wrinkles, smooth skin, add color, and trim chins. The average male has a 42-inch chest and a 34- to 36-inch waist. Male models usually have a 39-inch chest and a 30-inch waist.

Ads may be targeted at young children so they will ask their parents for certain foods. Companies sometimes use cartoon characters and toys to get the attention of young viewers. Eating food is fun and hip in advertisements made for teens. Many things, from cereal to macaroni and cheese, are seen in movies.

At the same time, the media show extremely thin, attractive people. The people in magazine ads, on television, and in movies often are eating unhealthy food. Somehow they stay thin and beautiful. People end up wanting the unhealthy foods they see on television. However, they also feel the need to look like the people they see in the media.

Points to Consider

What kinds of food choices are available in your home?

Can you think of a time when a friend said something about what you were eating? What was your reaction?

What are some ways you could make time for healthy eating during your day?

Chapter Overview

Healthy eating requires setting priorities, making decisions, and choosing nutritious foods.

Reading food labels can help in making nutritious food choices.

Setting long-term and short-term goals can help people live a healthy lifestyle. Journals and checklists can help them achieve their goals.

The body needs exercise almost as much as it needs food.

Chapter 7

How to Make Healthy Eating Part of Your Lifestyle

For most people, healthy eating means first changing the way they think about food and eating. The next step is to take action and change unhealthy eating habits and attitudes.

It's All in the Head

Healthy eating is about setting priorities and making decisions. The first step is to understand the importance of a healthy diet. It may be important to you to look and feel your best. If so, then eating right should be a priority, or an important matter. Most people want to live and enjoy a long life. Eating right can help accomplish this goal, too.

Eating right means choosing nutritious foods. The focus is not good foods versus bad foods. Instead, healthy eating is about including variety and balance in your diet. A balanced, healthy diet can include double-fudge brownies as long as it also includes vegetables, fruits, and grains.

Yvonne is comparing nutrition facts on toaster pastry and **YVONNE, AGE 18** multigrain cereal. Yvonne sees that the pastries have 5 grams of fat. That is 8 percent of the daily fat limit. The cereal has less than 1 gram of fat, or 1 percent of the daily value. The toaster pastry also contains 8 percent of the saturated fat for a typical diet. The cereal has none. Yvonne has cereal for breakfast. She knows this will help balance the cheese fries she will have for lunch.

Reading Food Labels

Food labels are a good source of information when making healthy eating choices. The government requires food labels to give the food's weight per package, ingredients, and nutrition information.

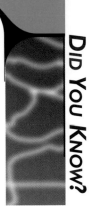
One of the most important dietary changes you can make is to limit the amount of high-fat foods that you eat. Balance your favorite high-fat foods with fruits, vegetables, beans, grains, and grain-based foods. Some grain-based foods are whole-wheat bread, multigrain crackers, and high-fiber cereals.

Since 1993, food labels have been required to show nutrition facts. These facts give the serving size and the number of calories per serving. They also list the amounts of certain nutrients found in the food. The label also shows the food's percentage of daily values. Daily values are recommended amounts of nutrients to be eaten daily. The percentage of daily values is helpful. It lets you know the contribution that a serving of the food makes toward your daily recommendation.

Long-Term Goals

Healthy eating should be part of an overall plan to improve well-being, or how you feel. Working to feel better, healthier, and more energetic may be a sensible, long-term goal. Eating right is the most important thing you can do to meet that goal.

Flexible, Short-Term Goals

Getting to a goal down the road can seem hard. It can be discouraging to think about what you have to do to reach that goal. The trick is to use short-term, mini-goals along the way. Accomplishing mini-goals can excite you about moving on. Before long, you will have made healthier eating a part of your life. You will have reached your goal.

The following mini-goals can help you meet a goal to live a healthy life:

Drink eight glasses of water each day.

Exercise at least 20 minutes 3 to 4 times each week.

Eat more vegetables and fruits.

Get plenty of sleep every night.

Mini-goals should be based on things that you have trouble doing now. If you already drink a lot of water, your mini-goal might be to eat fewer potato chips. When one mini-goal is met, move on to the next. Goals can be adjusted as your lifestyle changes. Writing down goals in a diary or notebook is helpful.

Journals and Checklists

Alex wants to try out for track in the fall. He thinks he needs

ALEX, AGE 14

to be in better shape. Alex bought a notebook and wrote down the date of track tryouts. Then he wrote down what he wanted to do before then to get in shape and feel better. He wrote, "Get plenty of rest, eat more veggies, ride my bike daily, and run five times a week." Every time Alex meets a mini-goal for a few weeks, he crosses it off his list. Sometimes he adds another short-term goal. Alex feels great. He knows he'll make the track team if he sticks to his plan.

Keeping a healthy eating journal can be as simple as writing a few things down in a notebook. Some people keep track of everything they eat and how much exercise they do. Some people write down how they feel when they eat, too.

Some experts recommend using a checklist every day. This is an easy way to make sure your diet is balanced. This food-choice checklist is based on the Food Guide Pyramid. The checklist doesn't have to be fancy. You could handwrite it and make photocopies. Or, you could type it on a computer and add your favorite clip art.

The checklist needs to have five headings: grains, vegetables, fruits, meats and meat substitutes, and milk foods. Next to each heading, put small boxes to represent each serving you should eat in a day. For example, vegetables would have at least three boxes and fruits would have at least two boxes. The number of servings, or boxes, depends on whether you are male or female. Chapter 4 gives information about the pyramid.

Each day, mark a box every time you eat a serving of food. By dinner, you will know what you still need to eat to balance your diet. Here's an example of what a checklist could look like.

Food Choice Checklist

Choice	Servings
Grains: serving size = 1 slice of bread, 1 ounce cereal, ½ cup pasta, or ½ roll or small bagel	☐ ☐ ☐ ☐ ☐ ☐ ☐ ☐ ☐
Vegetables: serving size = ½ cup cooked vegetables, 1 cup leafy greens, or ¾ cup juice	☐ ☐ ☐
Fruits: serving size = 1 medium piece of fruit, ¾ cup juice, or ½ cup canned fruit	☐ ☐
Milk foods: serving size = 1 cup low-fat or nonfat milk, 1 cup yogurt, or 1½ ounces cheese	☐ ☐ ☐
Meats and meat substitutes: serving size = 2 to 3 ounces lean meat; 1 ounce lean meat substitutes = 2 tablespoons peanut butter, 1 egg, or ½ cup beans or tofu	☐ ☐

Physical Activity

Physical activity is just as important as eating right. It helps people look and feel their best. The body needs activity almost as much as it needs food. Regular exercise helps lower cholesterol and increase energy. Unhealthy eating and no exercise are the two main things that lead to overweight, unfit teens and adults.

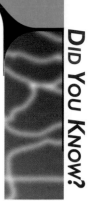
As children grow older, their level of activity drops. Boys at age 18 are 24 percent less active than when they were 6. A girl at age 18 is 36 percent less active than when she was 6.

One survey focused on Canadian girls ages 11 through 15. Of these girls, 25 percent said that, except for school, they were active one-half hour or less each week.

Being physically active does not just mean playing a sport or working out. It can mean working movement into your life every day. People can work many activities into their schedules. Like adults, teens should be generally active at least 30 minutes each day. Along with daily activities such as walking and doing chores, teens should exercise more heavily at least three times each week. Playing basketball, swimming laps, and climbing stairs are examples of this type of exercise.

Points to Consider

What are some priorities that you could set regarding the way you eat?

Why do you think the U.S. government requires food labels?

What are two long-term goals you have to improve the way you look and feel? What are three mini-goals for each long-term goal?

What kinds of things could people do to add activity to their daily schedule?

Chapter Overview

Eating right simply requires thinking about what you eat, planning meals, and making healthy choices.

It is important to start the day with breakfast.

Healthy snacks should be eaten every day.

Healthy eating may mean substituting some foods for others.

Chapter **8**

It's Easier Than You Think

Eating right is not difficult. However, it helps to think about what you eat, plan your meals, and learn to make healthy choices. You can do many things to help you feel better and have more energy. Some tips are included here to make it easier to eat healthfully.

Start the Day Right

Healthy eating includes eating breakfast. Breakfast jump-starts your body and your brain. It increases metabolism and energy. The body burns more calories all day long if a person eats breakfast. Eating breakfast helps the brain work better. It can help you do better in school and in sports.

Breakfast is important in making sure that teens get enough nutrients every day.

Eating breakfast improves test scores for some children and teens.

Breakfast foods that have some protein, a little fat, and naturally present sugars and unrefined starches give the longest lasting energy. They can help to get you through the morning.

You may not have time every morning to have a bowl of high-fiber cereal with fruit and milk. At least take the time to grab a cereal bar, some low-fat cheese, or a piece of fruit. Any of these foods gives long-lasting energy. Try to avoid doughnuts and other sugary breakfast foods. These give only short-term energy. You may find yourself dragging from class to class by midmorning.

Snack Attacks

Experts say snacks are okay. Snacks are a good way to provide energy between meals. Snacks satisfy hunger so you eat less at the next meal. However, eating a bag of chips and drinking cola is not a good idea. Healthy snacking means eating handfuls of food, not whole bags. Safe snacking also means eating nutritious foods such as whole grains, vegetables, fruits, and low-fat dairy products. It means avoiding too much fat and added sugars.

Some nutritious snacks are fruits, raw vegetables, yogurt, popcorn, frozen juice bars, and whole-grain cereals. Try to combine food groups when you snack. For example, eat carrots with peanut butter made from only ground peanuts and a little salt. Other snack ideas are multigrain crackers with low-fat cream cheese or yogurt with granola.

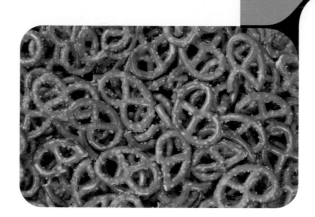

Substitutions

Often, eating right is just a matter of eating smaller amounts and substituting lower-fat choices for what you already eat. For example, drink 1-percent or skim milk instead of whole or 2-percent milk. Instead of ice cream, try nonfat or low-fat frozen yogurt. Pretzels are healthier than corn chips. You may have favorite foods that you can't easily replace with something else. These high-fat foods should be eaten only occasionally.

A Matter of Time

Many people share the same excuse for not eating right. They say they don't have time to fix healthier food. However, many foods at the grocery store are ready to eat and nutritious. The dairy and produce sections at your grocery store are good places to get quick snacks. Most stores have vegetables and fruit sliced and ready to go. Dried fruits, yogurt, and string cheese are more fast snacks. Whole-grain crackers and low-fat cheese work well, too.

Making Healthy Choices

Whether at a fast-food restaurant or at home, making healthy food choices is important. Most fast-food restaurants and food courts have nutritious food choices. Choose a smaller size rather than a super size. Baked, broiled, or grilled meat is better than fried. A salad with low-calorie dressing can help fill you up.

If you like Chinese food, stick to steamed rice and dishes with lots of vegetables. If you choose Italian food, try spaghetti with tomato sauce and added vegetables. Another option is plain spaghetti with a little parmesan cheese. You should ask for less sauce, if you are choosing a creamy alfredo sauce. A pizza slice with peppers, onions, and mushrooms goes great with a salad. Also, ask the server to have the pizza prepared with only half the cheese.

Bean burritos or chicken fajitas are good choices at a Mexican restaurant. Salsa or picante sauce adds even more flavor.

At the deli, try lean-meat sandwiches, such as turkey or roast beef, with light mayonnaise. Better yet, try replacing the mayonnaise with salsa or mustard. Ask for double lettuce and tomatoes. Go for onions and hot peppers if you are daring.

At home, grains, vegetables, fruits, low-fat milk, and lean meats should be the focus of meals. Choose grains such as brown rice, couscous, bulgar, quinoa, or wheat in the form of noodles. To the cooked grains, add vegetables and small amounts of lean meat or cheese. Bake, broil, or grill your meats. Fish and poultry such as turkey and chicken are good choices. Trim the fat from other meats. Fruit makes a nice side dish or dessert.

"My mom mixes pancake batter for our Sunday-morning breakfast. I cut up fruit and toss it in the batter. I get fruit, and the pancakes taste great. Little things like this can really add up."—Tim, age 14

"I really try to take time to eat meals with my family. We all help cook, and we take our time eating. We can't do it all the time, but I think we all eat better when we eat together."—Beata, age 17

N'CHELLE, AGE 15

"I thought I would never give up fast-food french fries. I was wrong. On weekends, I make a big batch of home fries. During the week, I heat them in the microwave. They're easy to make. I slice a few white and sweet potatoes into slivers and toss them into a bag with some seasoning. I use garlic powder, salt, and pepper. I remove the potatoes from the bag. Then I layer them on a cookie sheet coated with nonstick cooking spray. I bake them for 40 minutes at 350° or until golden brown. While they cook, I turn the potatoes a few times with a spatula."

Points to Consider

Do you think breakfast is important? Why or why not?

What are some substitutions you could do to make your diet healthier?

Do you have a favorite fast-food meal? What could you eat instead that would be more nutritious?

Glossary

artery (AR-tuh-ree)—a tube that carries blood from the heart to other body parts

calorie (KAL-uh-ree)—a measurement of the amount of energy that a food contains

carbohydrate (kar-boh-HYE-drate)—a nutrient that provides energy

cholesterol (kuh-LESS-tuh-rol)—a waxy substance made by animals, including humans, that is needed to make vitamin D, sex hormones, and other body chemicals

dietitian (dye-uh-TI-shun)—a person with education and special training about healthy eating and foods

digestion (duh-JESS-chuhn)—the process of breaking down food so the body can use it

disorder (DISS-or-dur)—an illness, sickness, or disease

esophagus (i-SOF-uh-guhss)—the tube that carries food and liquid from the throat to the stomach

fat (FAT)—an oily nutrient found in the body tissue of animals and some plants

metabolism (muh-TAB-uh-liz-uhm)—the process of changing food into energy

nutrient (NOO-tree-uhnt)—a substance in foods that is needed to help the body grow, stay healthy, and repair itself

nutritious (noo-TRISH-uhss)—health promoting

vegetarian (vej-uh-TER-ee-uhn)—someone who eats only plants and plant products and sometimes eggs or dairy products

vitamin (VYE-tuh-min)—a nutrient needed for growth and health

vitamin supplement (VYE-tuh-min SUHP-luh-muhnt)—a pill that contains vitamins

For More Information

Bennett, Paul. *Eating Healthy.* Parsippany, NJ: Silver Press, 1998.

D'Amico, Joan, and Karen Eich Drummond. *The Healthy Body Cookbook: Over 50 Fun Activities and Delicious Recipes for Kids.* New York: J. Wiley, 1999.

Krizmanic, Judy. *A Teen's Guide to Going Vegetarian.* New York: Viking, 1994.

Schaefer, Valorie Lee. *The Care and Keeping of You: The Body Book for Girls.* Middleton, WI: Pleasant Company Publications, 1998.

Zamorano, Ana. *Let's Eat.* New York: Scholastic, 1999.

Useful Addresses and Internet Sites

American Dietetic Association (ADA)
216 West Jackson Boulevard
Chicago, IL 60606-6995
1-800-877-1600 and
1-800-366-1655
www.eatright.org

Health Canada
Health Promotions and Programs Branch
Nutrition and Healthy Eating Program
Jeanne Nance Building, Tunney's Pasture
Ottawa, ON KLA 1B4
CANADA
www.hc-sc.gc.ca

U.S. Department of Agriculture (USDA)
Center for Nutrition Policy and Promotion
(CNPP)
Office of Public Information
1120 20th Street Northwest
Suite 200, North Lobby
Washington, DC 20036-3406
www.usda.gov/cnpp

U.S. Department of Health and Human
Services
Office of the Surgeon General
Office of Public Health and Science
Hubert H. Humphrey Building
200 Independence Avenue Southwest
Washington, DC 20201
www.surgeongeneral.gov/ophs

Vegetarian Resource Group (VRG)
PO Box 1463
Baltimore, MD 21203
www.vrg.org

Child and Family Canada
www.cfc-efc.ca/menu/eng008.htm
Provides access to various nutrition articles
from numerous organizations

The Healthy Refrigerator
www.healthyfridge.org
Has information and recipes for heart-healthy
eating and general nutrition for children and
teens

KidsHealth.org for teens
www.kidshealth.org/teen/
Provides information on health, food, and other
topics for children, teens, and parents

Nutrition on the Web (NOW!) for teens
library.advanced.org/10991/teen9.html
Interactive site created by teens for teens using
Mount Sinai Hospital nutrition information
and resources

Index

Index continued